POWER OF POETRY

ALPHABET CLUB

To the rebels, the dreamers, and the truth-seekers: may the power of poetry continue to inspire and ignite the fire within you. This anthology is dedicated to all those who have found solace, strength, and liberation in the words of the poets who have come before us and to those who will add their own voices to the chorus in the future. May these pages remind us of our humanity, our capacity for empathy, and our ability to create change through the power of language

Contents

Contents

Preface

"Power of Poetry" is a collection of poems that will take you on a journey through the human experience. These poems are not just words on a page, but a window into the hearts and minds of the poets who wrote them. These poems are a reflection of their lives, their struggles, their triumphs, and their hopes.

This anthology is a testament to the power of poetry to transcend time and place. These poems were written by poets from different eras and cultures, but they all speak to the universal human experience. They remind us that we are all connected, and that our struggles and triumphs are not unique to us.

The poets in this anthology have used their words to express the full range of human emotion, from love and joy to sorrow and despair. They have used their words to challenge societal norms and to speak out against injustice. They have used their words to inspire and to heal.

As you read these poems, you will be moved, you will be challenged, and you will be inspired. You will see the world through the eyes of these poets and you will be reminded of the power of poetry to change the world.

So, come on this journey with us, and discover the power of poetry. Let these words speak to your heart and your mind, and let them remind you of the beauty and the power of human expression. We hope that you will be inspired by these poems, and that you will be moved to write your own.

Thank you for joining us on this journey. We hope that you will be as moved and inspired by these poems as we were when we first read them.

~Alphabet Club Team

Acknowledgements

First and foremost, we would like to thank the members of the Alphabet Club for their hard work and dedication in creating this anthology. Their passion for poetry and their willingness to share their voices has made this book possible.

We would also like to thank our friends and family for their unwavering support and encouragement throughout the process of creating this book.

We are grateful to our editor for their guidance and expertise in shaping this anthology into a cohesive and meaningful collection.

Finally, we would like to thank our readers for their interest in the Power of Poetry and for supporting the work of the Alphabet Club. We hope that this book will inspire and uplift you, just as it has for us.

Prologue

Welcome to the Power of Poetry, an anthology of verse from the Alphabet Club. This collection is a celebration of the written word, showcasing the diverse voices and perspectives of our talented poets.

Our poets come from all walks of life, each bringing their own unique experiences and perspectives to the page. From the heart-wrenching to the humorous, these poems explore the depths of human emotion and the beauty of the world around us.

Whether you are a seasoned poetry aficionado or a newcomer to the genre, we invite you to dive into this anthology and discover the power of poetry for yourself. The words within these pages will inspire, challenge, and uplift you, and we hope they will leave a lasting impression on your heart and mind.

So turn the page and let the journey begin. We are honored to share these words with you and are confident that you will find something within them that speaks to you. Enjoy.

1. Mwana Wevhu

She is only an infant
But has succumbed to,
What adults have not,
Seen.
Withered cheeks, slim to
Almost skeleton point. She is
Only an infant, hunger devours her
Oh! Mwana Wevhu, why suffer like
The soil does?
So infertile, lack of nourishment, lives
In the streets alone. Why oh why did the
Dark hood choose such an infant?
Abandoned, forgotten, no one to take care
Of her. She has to be brilliant so as to be
Vigilant in this scavenger environment.
Oh Mwana Wevhu, she is only an infant!
Runganga Charity
Zimbabwe

2. Laughter in Pain

Beneath the many smiles
She has endless painful tears.
She hides them so well, but they have
A notorious habit of unveiling themselves
Oh! when will she know true joy?
Which many delight in, but it never seems to
Visit her side. When can it reach her heart?
She is lowly at heart and soft at heart, not
Much to offer, but surely she is a warrior.
One day, the happiness cloud will fall at
Her feet…
Runganga Charity
Zimbabwe

3. Need for Glory

She cries unto her Lord, she questions her
God. All she asks for is for him to shower
Love and mercy! She cries for peace, she
Cries for a new dawn.
She has been in the shadows of sorrow
For some time and she has not seen
What the glory and mercy feel like.
She cannot even express her agony,
All she does is cry and wish that
The light may visit her agony pit.
All our Lord, you will give her salvation!
Runganga Charity
Zimbabwe

4. Crown of Liberty

Once upon a time,

Mama Africa narrated,

My beauty had no competitor or battle,

Ebony queen makeup had no chance or space,

Blessed was my womb to give 54 unique kids,

Bonded with love and unified by 1500 languages, Mama owns,

The source of the world's longest river, the fantastic Nile,

Manifold species with spectacular colors,

Ancient mysteries of the Egyptian pyramids,

Masai Mara and Serengeti with scenery surpassing beauty,

I hear Victoria Falls whisper even 4 km away,

Beautiful sight of Mount Kilimanjaro with a fashioned ice cap on top,

Gemstone Tanzanite and unique Flora and fauna,

Our house is the year-round destination venue, brimming with visitors,

It offers culture heritage for tourists and attractions,

Ingrained sociopolitical and aesthetic values,

Tropical diseases give us a wakeup call to fight,

Sculptures and beadwork our badge of culture,

Ooh my hottest kids, Sahara and Al Aziziyah,

Ooh my fastest big five and fastest Kalenjin society,

Ancient Timbuktu paved a way for civilization,

Take care of your exquisite Mama Africa,

My kids, you are the formula for industrialization,

Democratization, and other unsolved equations,

I am the birth of mankind,

you are my genotype,

I shield you with the crown of liberty.

Angel Nanyaro

Tanzania

5. Votary of You

People around you define you,
They have great descriptions of who you are,
What they think about you isn't your concern,
Listen to them but learn to filter their words.
Let them talk,
Let them criticize,
You can't force them to validate you,
Their critics don't pay your bills.
For years, you have chosen them,
Just to fit into their shoes and be accepted by them.
My dear, you have to wake up,
It's time to learn to celebrate yourself,
It's time to acknowledge yourself,
You can't be shrinking to them,
You are worth and valued more than you think.
You're strong,
You're unique,
Give self-love a first priority,
Start to love yourself again,
You're responsible for your own happiness,
Valuing others is nice, but it begins with valuing yourself.

Angel Nanyaro
Tanzania

6. Love what you are positively Becoming !

Your castle needs a mason,
To build it strong and you are the mason,
You can decide to make it a villa or a mansion.
Journey is long,
Nuts are tight,
More battles to fight,
A lot of victories ahead,
While looking forward to what the future needs.
The door is open,
To allow their critics,
To allow their comments,
Their validation doesn't concern you,
Your personal approval is enough for now.
Let them murmur,
Cause you're evolving,
You're now transforming,
Let them bury your old version,
In the process,
you may not please everyone,
Just get to love what you are positively becoming,
You may not be their favorite hot soup during cold seasons.
While finding the new you,
It's not weird to lose some people,
Pains are inevitable in the mechanism,

Few will understand your transformation,

You have to bury and elude your information,

Accept the change and enjoy air with peace hands raised.

Angel Nanyaro

Tanzania

7. Swiping Left

That which I must do, to save my soul

For my heart, shall I do this

I won't compromise, to the pressures and pleasures I feel

If I make a mistake now, it will cost me my life.

It's the ticket I must take to agony, hell or the land of happy ever after

I am afraid of this,

The mistake I can't afford to make

I am left to say it's the matter, my feelings and emotions should be set aside

I need to use my brain and save my soul

It's the only guarantee

For which my hand gathers the strength to swipe left

The only room there is, to take the right direction

I can't afford this risk, it's a ticket to a lifetime decision

I am swiping left as an invitation to a glorious and happy lifetime!!

Love? Be it paradise or tragedy By swiping left, I foresee!!!

Evergrace Nibreny Aligawesa

Tanzania

8. Digging My Grave

It's the meal that felt so pleasing

The meal that I found ingredients so familiar

I can simply relate even to the cooking method

The simplicity of its baking method made it so real for me to get attached to

the result

I feel my emotions being pulled through

I could relate as a table was filled with all that is to do with my situations,

I could relate and feel

the pleasure of my feelings and emotions being communicated

I bet for some reasons I felt good about it

Others will say it's the wrong choice I made, to watch the negativity see them

portray my agony

They said I was pugnacious, getting ready to bombard the future

I beg to disagree, as I respond to pain and the agony I have been through in life

If I am being negative and feeding on the negativity, it's about the preparation. I think I need to be

bitter and treat life the same way it treated me

I presumed I was getting ready for the world's difficulties

Literally, I didn't know, I was setting my death patterns

I dug my own grave in a graveyard I helped prepare

I was already consumed by negativity and nothing was going my way

My brain was swept to think the opposite of the good in everything

I thought I was being real about life's situations and on guard, but, I

was rolling

in a pit, of an

agonized life

I clearly let my emotion and feelings take the lead and that's how the

fall

became of me

It's the meal I helped prepare by my own hands that poisoned me

It's in what I chose to feed in that consumed my thoughts

As I stand in the graveyard, I can spot out my grave. I chose the corner,

that

people can hardly spot

me

I embrace my trials, failures, and accept the burn to the afterlife

After I am cremated

I hope to be reborn and make amends!

Evergrace Nibreny Aligawesa

Tanzania

9. The Bench Mark

Their measure of excellence killed my spirit
I realized I had to give up right before I stared
This is not about the fear of taking risks
It's their wrong measurement of standards that compares subordinates inappropriately
How can you judge a fish by its ability to run on dry land?
They forget that we all move at different pace
We are all moving in different direction
They think their judgement is helpful
Little do they know they have demoralized us
It's not about the choice I have opted which is to give up
It's about the option they gave me, to fly yet they cut my wings long ago
I set my course as I value peace of mind, loosen the strings and detach myself
I am glad, I didn't put all my eggs in one basket
I choose to lay still like rivers crossing the mountains, you touch me once and I disappear, once
I have no doubt I'll come forth during the spring season
Just like a feather, I give my farewell and leave by the wind
Evergrace Nibreny Aligawesa
Tanzania

10. Burning faces

It's becoming harder and harder
To be a euphoric elated person
When all I want to do is cry
And sob
The heat dissipating from my sadness
Keeps burning the masks I have on for
People
It keeps interfering with the false portrayal
Of a joyous person I fool everybody with the mask
They think I am cheerful when I am desolate
They think I don't feel, whereas I feel way too
Much
I thought he could see behind the masks
When he looked at me I felt all my faces
Burning
I felt that finally someone could see me
But I was erroneous,
Absolutely mistaken
Surabhi Sharma
India

11. Cracks

You try to grow around the cracks in your soul,

But as you prosper,

The cracks start to whisper,

"You are still not enough, are you?"

You block the murmurs through loud music,

But your mind thinks,

"Am I crazy?" every time the music stops.

So you grow,

But the crevices grow with you.

Cracks turn into fissures,

Fissures turn into earthquakes,

Tearing down your heart and brain through and through.

Surabhi Sharma

India

12. Escapism

Depression is a boon I think

Poems, articles that I write are the collateral beauty

Resulting from years of trauma, damage, and deterioration

I put all of my tears, agony, torment in the words I write

Just so I don't feel them

It helps me show the world that I am apathetic

But in making people believe that I have no emotions

I fear I might actually have none left

Not even anger, shame, embarrassment. NOTHING

I am indifferent now

I don't care if the world ends tomorrow or if I have an assignment to complete

I cry just so I can feel human and alive

I fight to feel

I act happy to feel

But I am utterly and completely apathetic, indifferent towards the world.

Surabhi Sharma

India

13. Managing Emotions in a Love Triangle

Call me short-tempered because I'm short, but in the end, I would have shot

my shot.

It's not like I have a temper

That's about danger

To a stranger

It's all about the engagement of management, which is just inevitable.

Got me twisted in a

Twist of fate situation

Where a love triangle exists that keeps tangling into a tangle until we call it an entanglement.

Rugare Elgivva Takunda Jani

Zimbabwe

14. Crescent Hope

Hope is a thing with feathers
Not all feathers flock together
Pain demands to be felt
But the fault in our stars
Will not consider that
We live every day
And die once,
Wrinkles will never twinkle
Because the twinkle has become wrinkles.
Rugare Elgivva Takunda Jani
Zimbabwe

15. Mirage

I really wonder why
But never accept reality
Everything is so surreal
Yet so weirdly bizarre
I really need a bliss
But in the end it's a want
My want for luxury
Turns out to be very
Comfortable need I deserve
Being miserable is unbearable
Loneliness an instigator
Hard to digest
The end result is death
Just before the reach.
Rugare Elgivva Takunda Jani
Zimbabwe

16. 400+ years

It's been more than four decades and some change since someone saw his family.

He spent his whole life overworking in the factory.

Never saw lights, not even the day.

Tiredly working with the hardest clay.

It wasn't their choice to be there, neither was it a mistake.

They were captivated, chained, and even beaten to stay awake.

There were no freedom fighters and unfortunately they had no favor.

Molding bricks requiring many hours of labor.

Treated so badly for years, still endured the pain.

Some don't even know their homes, they've never had a view.

No one can help, they're all chained.

Zero freedom to step outside to see the morning dew.

They want to flee, the master is wicked and everyone fears.

When will these innocent people stop shedding tears?

Isaac Amo Essien

Ghana

17. The Youthful Message

Most of these skillful persons
Show nothing but life lessons.
People spend lots of money in space,
While others on earth end up in a rat race.
They pay no attention to the youth,
As if they're not part of the world.
This is what makes them loot.
How can they hear the wordless word?
Weren't we supposed to be born knowing all?
Some are growing wise, while others just grow tall.
Those here can't even be there,
Can we predict the future with a dare?
Aliens are credited for building the pyramids,
Pirates use the word "pillages" with ease,
But how can these captors invade villages with such ease?
They can't read the stars on their own,
Until the power and end of space is known.
This is the message our elders delivered to the kids,
They will one day leave the earth to see how space is.

Isaac Amo Essien

Ghana

18. Scars in Chasing

I am still chasing,

My heart stops at a point,

The race of difference needs,

A path that's far too lengthy and narrow to follow.

My face hit a wall,

Of ethnicity and language,

Their opposition aggressive,

But I smile with the face of a mother, and trudge through.

I have learned,

In every decision there is a race,

I am running the race,

Of language barriers,

Of racial conflicts,

Of color and political stagnation,

Of government and society.

Because a mother dreams,

She lives for the future of her children,

And I am one of them.

Christina Stokes

Ghana

19. Breaking

Trying so hard
To fix the dark strings
And the dark colors from
Stretching its vines
I fall in the process
My body failing me and
Its superior commands
The door is wide open with
No security making the space
Clueless
I still try to fight with my source
But it's shattering too
Not listening to its superior
Commands
I smile 'cause it seems I
Have the handles,
But within a fleeting lightning
moment I lose my hold
And am breaking
Losing all the colors and
Strings
Until one dominant color
Begins to spread its vines
Without fear and I'm reaching
Out to it

Until it's the only thing I

Can hold.

Christina Stokes

Ghana

20. Certain I might

Certain that as my body begs for the goodness of life
I am indeed needy of its salt
Certain that as my body begs for the goodness of life,
I am indeed needy of its salt,
Its dark chocolate, and perhaps its sourness.
I know, as I walk the grounds
Made of sand and rocks that
I might be someone's sinking ground.
Perhaps I might be someone's water,
Or I might replace the light of the lost street
Of the once ambitious Nkrumah.
Christina Stokes
Ghana

21. Love

Why love? Now see what you made me become. I am no longer myself anymore, it's like I exist now as a slave to you. I am no longer living by myself. Is this love that I hear of? If it is, then I'm giving up on you. I'm tired of moving from heart to heart. I am just a human being, why can't I have you entirely? The people you bring to me all destroy me in your name. They use you and I fall for it. Can't you see that I'm tired of being used because of your name? All are hiding their intentions, using your name. They come and immediately call upon your name and my heart opens up to them because, as they say, nothing is greater than love. You can't let this continue, love! You need to do something about it. Why do people prefer using you? You are always in front of every disappointment I get. Please don't let me lose hope in you. I'm scared that if I do, hate will replace you in my heart and if that occurs, there won't be any chance for you!

Samahan Namonje
Zambia

22. Mother's Love

Oh, mother, the most precious woman of all time, how can I even describe you? There is no description of you, mama. You loved me even before you knew of me. For over 9 months, you gave me room for me to grow in, not only that, you provided me with all the necessary things for me to develop. What a wonder you are, mama. During my stay for these 9 months, it wasn't easy. I led you to do things you weren't supposed to. You ate and napped all under my will, but every time you would lay your hand on my room and said you loved me. And when the time came for me to grow and breathe by myself, you opened up the door. During that time, I did not just leave the room willingly, but I kicked and gave you unbearable discomfort and pain. Your eyes were full of tears of pain, but as soon as you heard my cry, your face changed. There was a smile on your face, and as you held me into your hands, I looked into your eyes and all I could see was tears of joy. Oh, mother, what are you? I gave you pain and what I expected was hate, but you gave me unconditional love, where in the world will I ever find this compassion? Those sleepless nights don't matter. The room you gave me left a lot of marks on your body, every time you look in the mirror, you see those marks, instead of hurting you, smile and always feel proud of yourself that you gave me a chance. Oh, mother, how I love you! You are the best.

Samahan Namonje
Zambia

23. Suicidal thought

Suicidal thoughts, why me?

Why do you always come to me?

Why do you want me to give you my life?

Listen to me now, it's enough. I won't engage in any thought with you. Please quit, I am tired of you making me feel like taking my life is doing a favor to myself and those around me. You always manipulate me by saying nobody loves or cares about me. You are a liar, these people love and care. It's just because you are after my life that's why you feed me with all your lies. I won't give up on life. By now, you should know that I am not your slave anymore. Yes, you tell me that things won't get any better, but I have the answer to that. As long as I live, there is hope for everything around me to be better. You are after my life because you are so scared that if I live, I will win, for you know that I can only lose when I am dead. You are too late now because I have full knowledge about the power of life.

Samahan Namonje

Zambia

24. Sin

Can I ever escape you?
My burning desire to be blameless
Tirelessly, you bring me down
Sitting and knocking at my door
My flesh has partnered with you
No longer am I the master
You know that if I die, you burn with me.
Yet you rebel.
What sorrow awaits you!
Since you decided to part ways.
I choose the light, the true light.
That light shines in the darkness
And the darkness has not overcome it.
This light shall expose you!
This light gives life,
This light became flesh
And the flesh's blood
Made a way in the wilderness.
Now I'm on victory's side,
And you have been condemned.

Baiahun Talang
India

25. Your Only identity

Man, you are more valuable

Than the birds and the lilies of the valley.

Even in your sins, You are precious (More valuable than gold and silver).

Chance and a new beginning

You have been given.

Abandoning the fact that

Your creator is Holy and None like Him.

The universe bows down to Him,

The trees clap, the mountains burst into song.

The sky proclaims His handiworks.

The clouds are the dust of His feet

The host of heaven worships Him.

Unconditionally He loved, Humbly bore the cross.

How can you not see your value?

Baiahun Talang

India

26. Ironed with Love: A Tribute to Mothers

The warm smell of love
Lies on my ironed shirt.
She wakes up every day
Expressing love in many ways
Packing my lunch box,
Grooming my hair,
Keeping my shoes spotless,
Washing my clothes,
and Ironing my shirt.
She never rests
Until the evening, when she waits
To see me home safe again.
~to all mothers
Baiahun Talang
India

27. Life

Life is a journey,
So live it nicely,
Travel and enjoy,
As you ride the tide of life.
Life is a book,
You open a new chapter every day,
So read carefully as you go page by page.
Life is a ladder,
Climb one step at a time,
Be careful not to miss a step,
For your knowledge of steps helps in case of need.
Laetitia Makiwa
Zimbabwe

28. Death

Like a roaring lion,
Flashing like lightning,
Roaring like thunder,
Tearing like a whirlwind,
The memories are so vivid.
Flowing like a river,
Deeper than an ocean,
But higher than a mountain,
The sorrow is unbearable.
Gone without goodbye,
Forever without a call or message,
Thoughts so vivid,
Yet all are but memories.
Broken are the hearts left behind.
Coming back only in dreams,
Coming back only in memories,
To deepen the wound of sorrow,
To widen the gap of longing,
But all these are but memories only.
For you are gone,
Gone forever,
Never to be seen again,
Never to be heard talking,
But only memories.
Cruel death swallowed you,

Death devoured you,

Rain sealed your grave,

Grass grows to cover marks,

But only memories remain forever.

Laetitia Makiwa

Zimbabwe

29. My Bride

Gliding down the aisle,
Shining like a star,
With an innocent smile on her lips,
She looks at me through the corners of her eyes.
The crowd sighs with amazement,
Men whistle to themselves,
Women scratch each other,
But the look of innocence covers her face.
Soft as a cat's fur,
Innocent as a dove,
Graceful as a swan,
The look of innocence remains on her face.
Laetitia Makiwa
Zimbabwe

30. A Poem on Unrequited Love

To be honest,

I first felt attracted to you before I even knew you.

But I realized you didn't feel the same way,

So we decided to just be friends.

But I couldn't deal with my feelings for you,

So I hid them and pretended to be the perfect friend.

I went out and tried to find love elsewhere,

But it never worked out.

I was hurt and wanted to give up.

But then I saw you again,

And I realized you were always there.

Being with you feels like being with a part of myself.

I know now that you were meant for me,

I love you.

Michael Mugwenhi

Zimbabwe

31. A Son of the Soil's Journey

"Ladies and gentlemen, this is your captain speaking,"
Sounded a gentle but confident voice,
Of a dream that had become reality.
"Before we take off, please be reminded to fasten your seatbelt,"
Echoed yet again a confirmation that
This dream was no longer just a dream.
Mthulisi gazed through the aircraft windows,
A son of the soil now growing wings
Becoming a part of the family of flight.
Navigating with purpose, bearing heavily in his heart
His family's reputation and striving for success
With every breath taken, a goal achieved.
"Mthulisi, my child, etch your mother's wisdom deep within your heart,"
"Mthulisi, my child, etch your father's wisdom deep within your heart,"
Forget not the nest that fed you,
You are not a swift bird, But a stock bird,
You do not rest Until you reach the best.
"Though the winds may howl, the ravaging storm will soon come to a halt,"
Gently these words warmly infiltrated not his brain but his heart.
"Mthulisi, my son...", the flakes of memories from his greatest poet,
Kept on hugging his heart and he could do nothing but smile.

Michael Mugwenhi
Zimbabwe

32. Her Scream

Her scream peeled away her sunburnt dignity,

Robbing her of unfulfilling love,

A denial of a kiss that could heal her worries of tomorrow.

It stole an embrace of a loving family,

Her children sprouting from yonder,

He had scarred her body,

Smashing her soul and still warned her never to leave.

The children needed a mother,

And he still demanded a wife.

Wait - he is early today! Another shudder crawls across her skin,

Wrinkling it to the broken frame - the one that had caused her seven stitches,

Seven, resembling complete brokenness.

She could hear the leather belt unbuckle,

another scar she would endure…

Her scream made her swear on her innocence,

He staggers closer, reeking of alcohol,

smearing the kitchen walls with cheap perfume - he had hooked up with a woman at the tavern.

Such humiliation, building up her sorrow.

He didn't even look twice at her,

even though the fairytale had cut short.

Her barrenness had deprived her of a husband,

It came like lightning, and she melted to the floor.

Her body twitched in pain,

she ached to surrender as she watched them walk off to her matrimonial bed…

Her scream denied her of a choice

To keep herself pure until her prince charming rode along,

then at midnight their bodies would twine together and hold a sacred tale.

A father who was supposed to hand her over when she was ready,

had taken a bite himself. It came as a shame and dirtied her heels.

Her soles were muddied, her heart shattered,

Broken trust, broken homes, broken dreams.

As she swept the yard, she tried to sweep her pain away…

Her scream covered her with guilt,

She felt the blood sweep past her,

Blood of a life she had craved to hold,

And protect from the terror of the world,

The cry she had wanted to hear.

Blood that had become life within her,

She had sung to it by sunset and had risen by sunrise to quench its thirst for Amarula fruit.

He had forced her to abort - after all, no one would know.

He wasn't ready, and until he was, she had to be strong.

Yet this secret suffocated her,

Last year she had almost died…

Her scream buried her freedom,

Every woman was to be mutilated - was she an angel?

Her mother had looked at her with a strict warning that she was not supposed to whine and let alone try any tantrum over her genitals.

Women were tagged as submissive and that was prideful enough.

It came as a loud thrush of pain, a wailing of her womanhood.

Tears that would be regarded as a sin,

An atonement would be called for,

A peace offering for being afraid.

She lay in surrender, a broken vase seeking a potter…

Her scream meant nothing to him,

He had paid in full the dowry - a few cattle and a pot of salt.

A dedicated wife she was deemed to be,

age knew nothing, only love did.

A man should be fed and looked after regardless of her consent.

It came and broke her,

The soldier wanted to come for her next fall.

A decline to a desire to love willingly.

And as she said goodbye,

she felt the sun warm her coldness…

Her scream made her doubt him,

The words of love he had once echoed under the Musasa tree,

The letters he had written in the dimness

Panashe Munjoma

Zimbabwe

33. Jar of Ink

How much would a jar of ink cost?

I lost mine by the sea, whilst building sandcastles, infatuated and young.

And life was dripping honey, endorsed in silver roses.

Alas, at long last, I got a bee sting!

From where can I buy a jar of ink?

The other dried up, when I left it by the windowsill, drenched in agony to even close it.

I kept rolling back and forth, but the truth I knew: denial, dreams, naiveness.

Can I dip my pen in your ink?

The grey bottles smudged up, Stained my dreams, Smeared reality as luminescence,

But paved a truer path for me.

Where is an ink store nearer? Aunty Maggy took off with the yellow jar...

How much would a jar of ink cost?

I lost mine by the sea, whilst building sandcastles, infatuated and young.

And life was dripping honey, endorsed in silver roses.

Alas, at long last, I got a bee sting!

From where can I buy a jar of ink?

The other dried up, when I left it by the windowsill, drenched in agony to even close it.

I kept rolling back and forth, but the truth I knew: denial, dreams, naiveness.

Can I dip my pen in your ink?

The grey bottles smudged up, Stained my dreams, Smeared reality as luminescence,

But paved a truer path for me.

Where is an ink store nearer?

Aunty Maggy took off with the yellow jar...

Panashe Munjoma

Zimbabwe

34. Chronicles

I saw her by the gate,
Green meadow blushing her face away,
She wanted to ascribe to him,
Words only two hearts would enclose,
Ink only they would see.
She waved the paper wildly in the air,
And told me I was too young to understand,
Should I stray in pursuit?
"See, you are but a child, him you can't pursue,"
The may weather lightened her smile,
Even loose sandals she minded not.
He had tied her heart in a knot,
And today he would receive the note.
That, even today he still made her heart knock,
And she had yearned to.
She looked at me, giggled and turned away,
After all, I was a dote, such wasn't meant for years.
Whistle, let the postman hasten,
Such words should nestle him by day!
The dear child will dazzle!
Panashe Munjoma
Zimbabwe

35. Karma

For every bad deed,
a price must be paid.
In each sinful path,
Karma will be laid.
It matters not if the sins be small,
whoever is responsible,
Karma visits them all.
Kimberley Cheru
Zimbabwe

36. Humpty Dumpty

Humpty Dumpty sat on the wall,
Humpty Dumpty started to fall.
The crowd gasped, expecting a smash,
But Humpty hit the ground without a crash.
The crowd was shocked, even Old Jack,
Pondering why the egg did not crack.
Realization hit them, shock upon shock,
Humpty was not an egg, rather a smooth rock.
Kimberley Cheru
Zimbabwe

37. The Power of Love in the Journey of Life

In the romance of life,

We dance to the beat of our hearts.

With every step we take,

We find a new start.

With every breath we breathe,

We feel the passion grow.

And in the light of love,

We find a new glow.

Life is a symphony,

Of joy and sorrow.

But in the arms of love,

We find a brighter tomorrow.

With every beat of our hearts,

We feel the rhythm of life.

And in the power of love,

We find the strength to survive.

So let the romance of life,

Be the guiding light on your path.

For in the beauty of love,

We find the meaning of life at last.

Life is a beautiful journey,

With love as the treasure.

With every step we take,

Our hearts are filled with pleasure.

In the ups and downs,
We find our way.
With every laugh and tear,
Life's beauty comes to play.
With every new day,
We find a reason to live.
With every new dream,
We find the strength to give.
So let love be the compass
That guides you through life.
For in love's embrace,
We find the beauty of life.
Vinlaw Mudehwe
Zimbabwe

38. A Journey Through Time and Emotion

The poetry of life

Is written in the stars,

With every twinkle and shine,

A story begins and ends afar.

In the verse of life,

We find our purpose and rhyme,

With every step we take,

A new journey unfolds in time.

Life is a tapestry,

Woven with threads of love and pain,

But in the end, it's all worth it,

For it's the beauty that we gain.

With every word we write,

We pour out our hearts and souls,

And in the lines we create,

We find a new goal.

So let the poetry of life,

Be your guide through the years,

For in the verse of life,

We find the meaning and cheers.

Life is a melody

Of notes both sweet and sour,

With every verse we sing,

We find a new power.

With every line we write,

We pour out our souls,

And in the poetry of life,

We find our life's goal.

So let the poetry of life,

Be your guide in every step,

For in the verse of life,

We find our happiness.

Vinlaw Mudehwe

Zimbabwe

39. Love as a Firework: A Burst of Colors and Emotion

Love is a firework,
A burst of color and light,
It sets our hearts ablaze,
And makes everything feel right.
Love is a symphony,
A melody of the heart,
It fills our souls with music,
And sets us worlds apart.
Love is a treasure,
A precious gem to hold,
It shines bright and true,
And never grows old.
Love is a journey,
A path to explore,
With every step we take,
We find something more.
So let love be your guide,
Through the ups and downs,
For in love's warm embrace,
We find our true crown.
Vinlaw Mudehwe
Zimbabwe

40. Ego's Inferno: The Wilting of a Narcissist

But alas, the bloom was plucked,

By a narcissist's egotistical hand,

Leaving behind a trail of crushed petals and broken promises.

His ego, a towering inferno,

Consumed all that was pure,

Leaving nothing but ashes in its wake.

But as time passed and the ashes settled,

The true colors of his deceit were revealed.

His once charming words, now empty echoes,

His once loving touch, now a distant memory.

And as he watches from afar,

The flower that he once destroyed,

Blossoms once again, in the arms of another.

He realizes too late, the beauty he had,

And the love he let slip through his grasp.

He mourns the loss,

of what could have been,

But the flower has moved on,

And he is left to wilt in his regrets.

Kelvin Saungweme

Zimbabwe

41. Anchored in Love

In the depths of my despair,
I tread the turbulent sea,
Of emotions that swirl,
And threaten to engulf me.
In the darkness of my mind,
My thoughts are twisted and torn,
But your love is a beacon,
That guides me through the storm.
With every wave that crashes,
I feel my strength slip away,
But your hand reaches out,
And pulls me back to day.
In the deep murky waters,
I lose my way,
But your love is my anchor,
That keeps me safe and saves me.
With your touch,
the clouds clear,
And the sun shines bright,
In your arms,
I find peace,
And all my fears take flight.
With your love,
I am saved,
From the depths of my despair,

And my soul is lifted,

To a love beyond compare

Kelvin Saungweme

Zimbabwe

42. Dear Daisy: Eternally Yours

To fill my heart with your essence.

My love for you is a tempestuous storm,

that rages within my soul.

It's a fire that burns with a fierce intensity,

a never-ending, insatiable goal.

Your eyes are like the ocean,

deep and vast,

I long to dive into their depths,

and be forever lost.

My love for you is a grand parade,

but it's not filled with flowers or noise,

it's a grand parade of emotions,

that will forever be my joys.

I love you as the morning sun,

that warms my frozen heart,

I love you as the light that guides me,

when I'm lost in the dark.

I love you without warning,

with a passion that knows no bounds,

I love you with a tender touch,

that shakes me to the ground.

I love you with a loyalty,

that will last until the end of time,

I love you now,

I loved you then,

and I will love you forever and a lifetime.

In your silence,

I hear your voice,

in your absence,

you are forever present,

One word, one smile,

is all it takes,

to fill my heart with your essence.

My love for you is infinite,

eternal, and true,

I will love you forever,

that's all I want to do.

Kelvin Saungweme

Zimbabwe

43. Navigating the Minefield of Love

I am the minefield of love, a treacherous path to tread

Each step a gamble, each move a risk to be made

Some say I am a curse, a trial to be endured

But to those who brave my dangers, they know the allure

I am the thrill of the chase, the fire in the heart

I am the rush of emotion, the work of art

I am the test of trust, the measure of devotion

I am the challenge of the heart, the ultimate emotion

I am the road less traveled, the path of the brave

I am the one that will test you,

push you to your limits, to see what you can achieve

But with each step, with each breath, I bring you closer

To the one you have always been searching for

I am the minefield of love, a field of battle

But for those who can navigate me, I am the key to the castle

I am the possibility of true love, the joy of companionship

But I come with warning, one false move and you'll be done with.

So tread lightly, with caution, with care

And maybe, just maybe,

you'll find love waiting there.

David Nemaungwe

Zimbabwe

44. Everlasting Love

The hope we had is fighting through our hands like sand

But still we hold on tight, not wanting to let go of our plans

We've been through the storms, the winds, the rains

But our love remains, a burning flame that sustains

We've built our castle in the sky, brick by brick

With every kiss, every touch, every beat of our hearts quick

We've etched our names in the stars, forever entwined

Our love a tale of the ages, a love that is one of a kind

We've danced in the moonlight, whispered sweet nothings in the dark

We've laughed, we've cried, we've left our mark

But through it all, through the highs and the lows

Our love continues to grow, a never-ending rose

So let the hope we have fight through our hands like sand

For in the end, our love will forever stand.

David Nemaungwe

Zimbabwe

45. The Journey of Life and Strength

Life is a journey, winding and long
With hills to climb and valleys to pass along
But with each step we take, we grow stronger still
Forging our own path, with will and skill
We all have our struggles, our battles to fight
But it's the way we face them that sets us alight
For in the darkest of days, and the stormiest seas
We find the strength to rise above and be free
For life is not easy, but it's worth the fight
For every tear shed, there's a ray of light
And in the end, it's not the victories we've won
But the strength we've gained and the battles we've overcome
So stand tall, my dear, and face the world with grace
For you are a warrior, with an unbreakable face
For every wound you bear, and every scar you show
Is a testament to the strength that you know
For life is a journey, and we are all on the way
With our own paths to tread and our own struggles to face
But in the end, it's not the destination we seek
But the strength we gain, and the lessons we learn on the way

David Nemaungwe

Zimbabwe

Index

Author : David Nemaungwe

Special Thanks!

Alphabet Club would like to extend our heartfelt thanks to all of the poets who contributed to Power of Poetry anthology. Your words have brought beauty and depth to the pages of this book, and we are honored to have your work represented here.

We would also like to thank our readers for taking the time to explore the Power of Poetry. We hope that this collection has inspired and uplifted you, and that it will serve as a reminder of the power of poetry to connect and transform us all.

This anthology features the works of the following poets:

- Runganga Charity -Zimbabwe
- Angel Nanyaro -Tanzania
- Evergrace Nibreny Aligawesa -Tanzania
- Surabhi Sharma -India
- Rugare Elgivva Takunda Jani-Zimbabwe
- Laetitia Makiwa -Zimbabwe
- Michael Mugwenhi -Zimbabwe
- Panashe Munjoma -Zimbabwe
- Samahan Nanjome -Zambia
- Kimberley Cheru -Zimbabwe
- Christina Stokes - Ghana
- Isaac Amo Essien-Ghana
- Baiahun Talang -India
- Kelvin Saungweme -Zimbabwe
- David Nemaungwe- Zimbabwe
- Vinlaw Mudehwe -Zimbabwe

We encourage you to learn more about these poets and their other works, as well as to explore other poetry collections and resources.

We also invite you to submit your own poetry for consideration in future anthology editions by Alphabet Club.For future submissions, please email us at **poetryanthalogy22@gmail.com** or follow us on social media [**instagram @alpha_betclub** & **facebook page @ Alphabet Club**]for updates on future publications and submissions.

We are excited to announce that we have recently opened a club apparel store where you can purchase clothing and accessories with designs inspired by the poetry featured in this anthology. It is a great way to show off your love for poetry and support the club at the same time. You can find the store at **www.alphabetclub.shop.**

Finally, we would like to extend our gratitude to our editors, for their tireless work in curating and organizing this anthology aswell as our creative design team for their efforts in bringing this book to life.

Thank you for being a part of the Power of Poetry by Alphabet Club. We hope you will continue to enjoy and appreciate the beauty of poetry in the future.

Yours Sincerely,
Alphabet Club

Scan & Join